The World Needs A UNIQUELY HAPPY YOU!

WRITTEN BY MAKIDA ARSHI

ILLUSTRATED BY SIDDHANT JUMDE

To my daughters Hira Yussuf, Nina Yussuf, and Ayah Yussuf: This book wouldn't be possible if you didn't choose me to be your mother. You inspire me every day. You make life fun. I love you forever, I'll like you for always. As long as I'm living my baby you'll be.

To my nieces Derartu, Noor, Niyyana, Ayla, Tesnim, Hanim, Siham, Judy, Hanim Shafi, Adila Shafi, Nicoterisa, Abigail, Ema, Hanah, Maya, and Gabby: This book is for you too. Aunty loves you so much.

To my husband Ismael: I appreciate you and your unwavering support.

Great load of thank-you to my parents, siblings, and friends.

And thanks to my editorial and production team at **Bear With Us Productions**.

Published in association with Bear With Us Productions
www.justbearwithus.com

979-8-9870882-0-3

The World Needs A UNIQUELY HAPPY YOU!

WRITTEN BY MAKIDA ARSHI

ILLUSTRATED BY SIDDHANT JUMDE

In a town not far from here,
There lived a group of friends,
They all had *different heritage*,
And very different ends.

And, though the friends were very close,
They were not all the same –
Each one had her *hopes* and *dreams*
For when the future came.

These American-born girls
Had parents from all nations,
Whose languages and cultural pride
Passed down the generations.

The girls had seen the misery
That modern life could bring,
They saw that women had no chance
Of doing their own thing.

If they chose career or kids,
To marry, or stay alone,
Nothing really satisfied,
Someone would always moan!

And so, the friends all made a pact
To live life as they pleased,
They would never drop their dreams,
Or leave a chance unseized.

For every girl deserved to grow
Into a woman blessed,
To be themselves, inside and out,
To be *them* at their best.

So . . .
I bet you all are wondering
What they grew up to be.
Well, turn the page to meet the gang
And hear each girl's story.

Smart with kind heart,
Selam's gift was healing,
If kids were hurt or miserable,
She'd know how they were feeling.

For Selam, helping people
Was her greatest joy and skill,
She knew she'd get the best grades,
With her *focus*,

brains,

and *will*.

In twenty years, she's grown up,
Just look at what she's done!
A doctor, as she dreamed of,
And loved by everyone.

Curing sickness,
stitching cuts,
Treating all with care,
She does the job she loves each day,
With *passion*,
pride,
and *flair*.

Priya's proud parents
Never could deny
That all she'd ever wanted
Was to fly *high* in the sky!

All through school and growing up,
Priya used her brains,
And trained to be a pilot,
Flying huge airplanes.

But when her children came along,
She found a brand-new dream,
She gave up work to stay at home –
Her mom skills are supreme!

Arezo, a creative girl,
Was brilliantly artistic.
She hoped her art would change the world,
And she stayed optimistic.

She drew in *pencil*, *chalk*, and *ink*,
Dashed paint on floors and walls,
She covered every surface
With her amazing scrawls.

Now, here she is, in her own shop,
Selling her creations,
The joy she gets from sharing them
Exceeds her expectations!

Her work lights up the houses
Of her customers, for sure;
If ever they are feeling sad,
Her paintings are their cure.

As a kid, Diana loved
To give her classmates cheer,
Inspiring other people
Was her *ideal career*.

Motivational speaking
Is where her passion led;
People turn up feeling sad,
And leave happy instead.

Izabel, a caring girl,
Looked after dolls all day,
Feeding, teaching, rocking them,
Oh, how she loved to play!

She grew up and decided
A "career" was not for her,
To stay at home,
and be a mom,
Was what she would prefer.

And here she is, with seven kids!
A supermom, no doubt,
With no regrets at opting
For a "stay-at-home-mom" route.

Nobody made her do this,
It was her *wish*,
her *choice*,
She's happy as the day is long –
Her kids make her rejoice!

Her parents were so curious,
That Li loved information,
To find out about everything
Gave her the best sensation.

She read big books,
searched far and wide.

To learn all that she could,
And took the knowledge that she found
Into her adulthood.

And to this day, to search for facts
Is still her favorite task,
And luckily, facts are her job.
"What does she do?" you ask.

She does research and works from home
In her one-person house,
And Li adores her solo life —
No *kids*,

no *pets*,

no *spouse*.

Chelsea loved explaining things
To other kids at school,
To help them understand ideas,
Or some new fact or rule.

She still loves kids, now she's grown up,
But has none of her own,
For she prefers to teach them,
Then to leave work and go home.

She loves expanding bright young minds,
And helping kids who struggle,
But at home, with her husband near,
She likes her tranquil bubble.

Alex loved a great debate,
Of that, there was no doubt,
If somebody did something wrong,
She'd quickly point it out.

She always had a passion
To change things for the better,
And, with her speeches and campaigns,
She was a fierce go-getter!

She's a congresswoman now,
And gets to make the laws,
Working hard with all her strength
To aid each noble cause.

Perhaps one day she'll be in charge –
Who knows? No one can say,
Her goal is to be president,
And lead the USA.

For the adventurous Ada,
Space was the first love,
She yearned to journey to the moon,
And all the stars above.

Ada walked around all day,
Her head in a fishbowl.
"I'm a space girl!" she'd announce –
Yep, space was in her soul!

If you look for Ada now,
You won't find her down here,
She lives on a space station
For six months of the year.

As she looks down from high above –
A view that she enjoys –
She revels in her silent home:
No *cultures*,
race,
or *noise*.

And, though they live such diverse lives,
The group remains great friends,
Their love and admiration
For each other never ends.

Right now, they have a message
That they'd like you to hear,
A message to remember
When your journey seems unclear . . .

Grow up and be happy,
Do what you want to do,
Because the world is richer with
A uniquely happy you!

About the Author

Makida Arshi is both an author and a full-time nurse from Virginia. She is of Ethiopian descent and lives with her husband, Dr. Ismael Yussuf, and her three wonderful daughters Hira, Nina, and Ayah.

She has always struggled with the societal expectations of women. At certain points, she has had to make the choice between working, staying at home to look after her children . . . or both! In making those choices, she has often found that whichever one she made, there would always be some part of society that would have a problem with it. Makida hopes to be instrumental in dismantling such expectations of women across the world.

This is why she saw the need to write a book to encourage young readers, girls in particular, that it is OK to be what they choose to be as long as they are happy doing it, to embrace who they are and live their truth.

Made in the USA
Middletown, DE
30 September 2023